ABHINANDAN PATIL

Application of CPlusPlus for Practical Problems

Copyright © 2023 by Abhinandan Patil

All rights reserved. No part of this publication may be reproduced, stored or transmitted in any form or by any means, electronic, mechanical, photocopying, recording, scanning, or otherwise without written permission from the publisher. It is illegal to copy this book, post it to a website, or distribute it by any other means without permission.

First edition

This book was professionally typeset on Reedsy.
Find out more at reedsy.com

To My Wife Sangeeta and My Kids Ishan and Shivansh.

There is no alternative to hard-work and perseverance.

— Abhinandan H. Patil

Contents

Preface	ii
Acknowledgement	iii
About the Author, Me	iv
Chapter 1: Starting the Journey of C++	1
Chapter 2: Installation of C++ on Your System or Using…	2
Chapter 3: Some Simple Problem Definitions and Their…	5
Chapter 4: Some More Simple Problems Solved	11
Chapter 5: Some Moderate Problems Solved	19
Chapter 6: Some Pointers Please. Including Copy Constructors	27
Chapter 7: Inheritance, Virtual Functions and Run Time…	40
Chapter 8: Where to Go from Here?	64

Preface

This book is totally informal and unconventional in its approach. Theory text is kept bare minimal. Targeted readers of this book are intermediate C++ programmers. This book is definitely not for novice programmers. However, Authors mentions about some Authoritative books by other competent Authors for beginners. The Author takes application of learned concepts approach and does not start with introduction to C++. This book contains 20+ practical problems and their solutions. Author liberally uses his own notes that he used for teaching at Universities. The Author strongly asserts his copyright over every content in this book that he prepared for teaching. This book is lab oriented and tests you on your learned concepts. After solving all the problems you should have gained some knowledge in C++. Good luck!.

Acknowledgement

First of all many thanks to Reedsy for giving me a software where type setting and formatting is breeze. Many Thanks to Microsoft Corporation for the wonderful OS Windows 11 with add on utilities. Also thanks to Microsoft Corporation and Open source community for VSCode and its extensions. Daniel Pintoo your extension for VSCode is amazing. Many Thanks to g++, gdb communities. MSys2 project needs shout out for making g++,gdb available on Windows. Ms Word was used for Mathematical expressions. Office 365 team needs special mention. Applications such as Okular, Snipping Tool were very handy. Dell Corporation and HP need a mention for giving wonderful hardware.

Finally Author thanks other Authors whose material is readily available for C++ learners.

About the Author, Me

I am a proud global citizen and published teacher with 3 Udemy courses, 15 Books, open access Blog and open access YouTube channel.

I can teach Computational Mathematics, Data Science, ML/DL, Internet of Things, Programming languages, Web technologies, Cloud Computing, Microcontrollers, Electronics for Computer Scientists, Operating Systems, Computer Networks, Data Structures and Algorithms, Software Engineering and Software Testing.

I am Author of 15 Books and 14 Scientific Articles. I am Life-Long learner with **many** areas of interests. Earlier, I have worked in Wireless Network Software Organization as Lead Software Engineer for close to a decade. I was in **USA** for two long stints and was instrumental in Releases of Mobility Manager at Motorola USA as Single Point of Contact for Network Simulator Tool. My Research is available as Books and Thesis in IJSER, USA. My Thesis published as Book is rated as one of the best Books of all time for Regression testing by **BookAuthority.org**. I am an Active Researcher in the field of Computational Mathematics, Machine Learning, Deep Learning, Data Science, Artificial Intelligence, Regression Testing applied to Networks, Communication and Internet of Things. I am an active contributor of Science, Technology, Engineering and Mathematics. I am currently working on few Undisclosed Books. I have started Blogging recently on Technology and Allied Areas. I have been National and International awardee. I am Senior IEEE member since 2013 and member of Smart Tribe and Cheeky Scientists Association. I am UGC-NET Qualified (2012). Recipient of several Bravo awards for deserving work at Motorola. I am on the Editorial Board of few Scientific Journals. I am an ardent reader of **STEM(Science, Technology, Engineering and Mathematics)**. I have desire to contribute more to STEM.

More details about me at: **https://abhinandanhpatil.info/**

Chapter 1: Starting the Journey of C++

Some great resources for C++

1. Modern C++ for Absolute Beginners by Slobodan Dmitrović
2. Beginning C++17 or C++20 by Ivor Horton and Peter Van Weert
3. Clean C++ by Stephan Roth
4. SamsTeachYourself C++ by Siddhartha Rao
5. Object oriented programming in C++ by Robert Lafore
6. The C++ Standard Library by Nicolai M. Josuttis
7. Working draft, Standard for C++ programming language, latest

I do not intend to replicate the material already documented in authoritative documents by technically competent Authors mentioned above. Rather my approach is to give a practical problem description and solve it. I use my own notes which I prepared for teaching C++ in Universities. I also re-use my code which I developed for teaching C++ at Universities. I strongly assert that all the content in this book is created by me.

Chapter 2: Installation of C++ on Your System or Using Online C++ Compilers

You could chose to install:

1. g++
2. MSVC++
3. LLVM Clang

On Windows/Linux/Mac as the case may be. You could choose to use Professional IDE such as MSVSCode with its extensions.

If you happen to use Windows and decide to go with g++ and VSCode, https://www.msys2.org/ is great resource for installing g++ and gdb.

You must see the following on your command prompt

CHAPTER 2: INSTALLATION OF C++ ON YOUR SYSTEM OR USING...

```
Windows PowerShell
Copyright (C) Microsoft Corporation. All rights reserved.

Install the latest PowerShell for new features and improvements! https://aka.ms/PSWindows

PS C:\Users\WELCOME> g++ --version
g++.exe (Rev10, Built by MSYS2 project) 12.2.0
Copyright (C) 2022 Free Software Foundation, Inc.
This is free software; see the source for copying conditions.  There is NO
warranty; not even for MERCHANTABILITY or FITNESS FOR A PARTICULAR PURPOSE.

PS C:\Users\WELCOME> gdb --version
GNU gdb (GDB) 12.1
Copyright (C) 2022 Free Software Foundation, Inc.
License GPLv3+: GNU GPL version 3 or later <http://gnu.org/licenses/gpl.html>
This is free software: you are free to change and redistribute it.
There is NO WARRANTY, to the extent permitted by law.
PS C:\Users\WELCOME>
```

Command Prompt or PowerShell Sanity Check

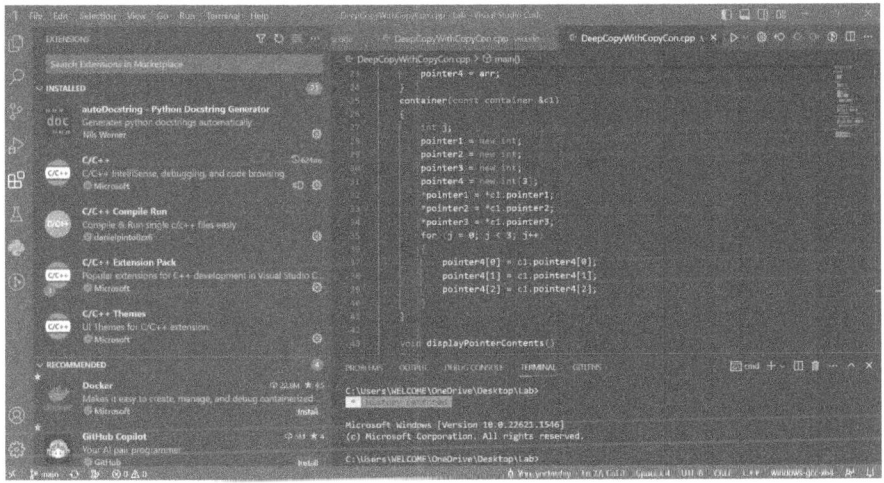

MSVSCode Extensions

3

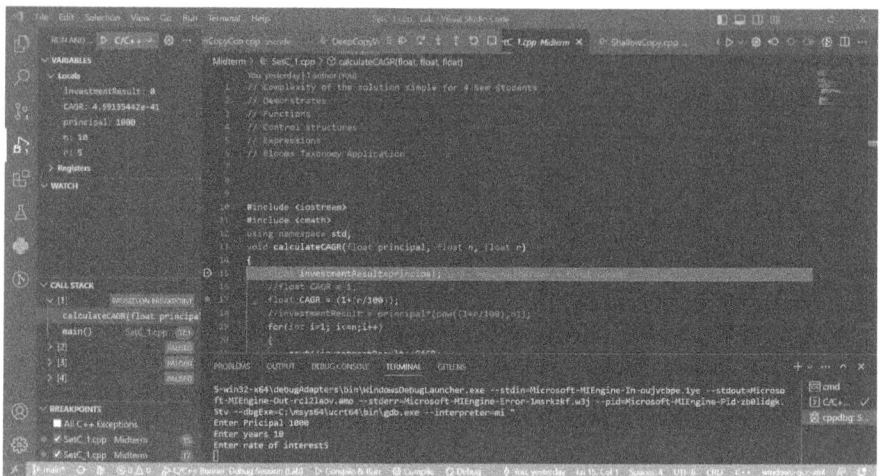

Sanity check for Debugger Setup

Chapter 3: Some Simple Problem Definitions and Their Solutions

From permutation combination theory,

$$C_r^n = \frac{n!}{r!(n-r)!}$$ Where Mathematical notation n! is n factorial calculated as n*(n-1)*(n-2)………*2*1

You are supposed to accept the values n and r from input stream in driver code. Classes and objects are optional. However, factorial must be a function and nCr must also be function. The calculated value of nCr must be printed to output stream meaningfully.

Problem Definition for NCr

Program for the above mentioned Problem Definition

```
// Demonstrates
// Functions
// Control structures
// Expressions
// Blooms Taxonomy Application
#include <iostream>
using namespace std;
int fact(int n)
{
```

```
  int result=1;
  while(n != 1)
  {
     result= result * n;
     n=n-1;
  }
  return result;
}
int ncr(int n, int r)
{
  int result=1;
  return (fact(n)/(fact(r)*fact(n-r)));
}
int main()
{
  int n=0,r=0;
  cout<<"Enter the values of n and r separated by space ";
  cin>>n>>r;
  cout<<n<<"C"<<r<<"is"<<ncr(n,r);
}
```

Output

```
Enter the values of n and r separated by space 5 2
5C2is10
```

CHAPTER 3: SOME SIMPLE PROBLEM DEFINITIONS AND THEIR...

Create two arrays of Strings representing two Mathematical sets where each individual element of an array represents the individual element of set. Then find the cartesian product using Mathematical set theory. Classes and Objects optional. Cartesian product calculation must be via function.

Example:

Set1 = { Red, Blue}

Set2 = { Bag, Coat, Shirt}

Cartesian Product of Set1 and Set2 is

(Red,Bag), (Red,Coat), (Red,Shirt), (Blue,Bag), (Blue,Coat), (Blue,Shirt)

Problem Definition for Cartesian Product of Two Sets

Program for the above mentioned problem

```
// Demonstrates
// Functions
// Control structures
// Expressions
// Pointers
// Blooms Taxonomy Application

#include<iostream>
using namespace std;
void cartesianProduct(string* a, int m, string* b, int n)
{
   int i,j;
   for (i=0; i<m; i++)
   {
      for(j=0;j<n;j++)
      {
         cout<<"("<<a[i]<<","<<b[j]<<")";
      }
   }
}
int main()
{
```

```
    const int N = 10;
    int m=0,n=0,i=0,j=0;
    string a[N];
    string b[N];
    cout<<"Enter how many elements in first set?";
    cin>>m;
    cout<<"Enter how many elements in second set?";
    cin>>n;
    cout<<"Enter the first set";
    for(i=0;i<m;i++)
    cin>>a[i];
    cout<<"Enter the second set";
    for(j=0;j<n;j++)
    cin>>b[j];
    cartesianProduct(a,m,b,n);
}
```

Output:

```
Enter how many elements in first set?2
Enter how many elements in second set?3
Enter the first setRed Blue
Enter the second setHat Coat Gloves
(Red,Hat)(Red,Coat)(Red,Gloves)(Blue,Hat)(Blue,Coat)(Blue,Gloves)
```

CHAPTER 3: SOME SIMPLE PROBLEM DEFINITIONS AND THEIR...

You are working for bank as programmer for a day. Your client visits you and wants to know how his/her investment Principal(P) grows over period of time N years in your bank where your bank compounds investment annually using the following formula.

Investment worth at the Nth year is $P(1 + \frac{r}{100})^N$ where P is Principal, r rate of interest

So your program should print table as follows

Your investment of 1000 with 5% compound interest is 1050 after 1 year
Your investment of 1000 with 5% compound interest is 1102.5 after 2 years
....

....
Your investment of 1000 with 5% compound interest is 1628.8 after 10 years
You must use function for calculating the investment growth. Classes and objects optional.

Investment Growth Problem Definition

Program for the above mentioned problem

```
// Demonstrates
// Functions
// Control structures
// Expressions
// Blooms Taxonomy Application



#include <iostream>
#include <cmath>
using namespace std;
void calculateCAGR(float principal, float n, float r)
{
   float investmentResult=principal;
   //float CAGR = 1;
   float CAGR = (1+(r/100));
   //investmentResult = principal*(pow((1+r/100),n));
   for(int i=1; i<=n;i++)
```

```cpp
    {
      cout<<investmentResult<<CAGR;
      investmentResult = investmentResult*CAGR;
      cout<<"Your investment of "<<principal<<"at ";
      cout<<r<<"interest percent is"<<
      investmentResult<<"is"<<i<<"years later";
      cout<<endl;
    }
}
int main()
{
  float principal,n,r;
  cout<<"Enter Pricipal ";
  cin>>principal;
  cout<<"Enter years ";
  cin>>n;
  cout<<"Enter rate of interest";
  cin>>r;
  calculateCAGR(principal,n,r);
}
```

Output

```
Enter Pricipal 1000
Enter years 10
Enter rate of interest5
Your investment of 1000at 5interest percent is1050is1years later
Your investment of 1000at 5interest percent is1102.5is2years later
Your investment of 1000at 5interest percent is1157.62is3years later
Your investment of 1000at 5interest percent is1215.51is4years later
Your investment of 1000at 5interest percent is1276.28is5years later
Your investment of 1000at 5interest percent is1340.1is6years later
Your investment of 1000at 5interest percent is1407.1is7years later
Your investment of 1000at 5interest percent is1477.46is8years later
Your investment of 1000at 5interest percent is1551.33is9years later
Your investment of 1000at 5interest percent is1628.89is10years later
```

Chapter 4: Some More Simple Problems Solved

To find Triangle is equilateral, isosceles or scalene triangle.

[Geometry basics: If all sides are same then is equilateral triangle. If two sides are same then it is isosceles. If all the sides are different, then it is scalene]

Create a class triangle. Set method should set sides a, b and c respectively via cin. Then type of triangle method should print the type of triangle as per the geometry basics explained above.

Also write the expected output for your program execution.

Solution to the above mentioned problem

```
#include <iostream>
using namespace std;
class triangle
{
  int side1,side2,cide3;
  public:
  void getSides()
  {
    cout<<"Side 1 :"<<endl;
    cin>>side1;
    cout<<"Side 2 :"<<endl;
    cin>>side2;
    cout<<"Side 3 :"<<endl;
```

```cpp
    cin>>side3;
  }
  void typeOfTriangle()
  {
    if (side1 == side2 && side2 == side3)
    {
      cout<<"Triangle is equilateral"<<endl;
    }
    else if (side1 == side2 || side2 == side3 || side1 == side3)
    {
      cout<<"Triangle is isosceles"<<endl;
    }
    else
    {
      cout<<"Triangle is scalene"<<endl;
    }
  }
};
int main()
{
  triangle triangleType;
  triangleType.getSides();
  triangleType.typeOfTriangle();
}
```

Output:

```
>
Side 1 :
5
Side 2 :
4
Side 3 :
4
Triangle is isosceles
>
Side 1 :
5
```

CHAPTER 4: SOME MORE SIMPLE PROBLEMS SOLVED

```
Side 2 :
5
Side 3 :
5
Triangle is equilateral
```

Distance of given point from origin

Create Class Point. It should have x,y cartesian co-ordinates as data members. The distance r should also be data member. Then there should be set method to set x and y. The calculate distance of point from the origin uses Pythagorean formula. That is distance r is sqrt(x*x + y*y). Further display method should display cartesian co-ordinates x,y and distance r in meaningful manner.

Also write the expected output for your program execution.

Solution to the above mentioned problem

```
#include <iostream>
#include <cmath>
using namespace std;
class point
{
private:
  int x, y;
  float r;

public:
  void setxandy()
  {
    cout << "Enter x:" << endl;
    cin >> x;
    cout << "Enter y:" << endl;
    cin >> y;
  }
  void calculateDistance()
```

```
    {
       r = sqrt(x * x + y * y);
    }
    void display()
    {
       cout << "x and y are: " << x << " and " << y << endl;
       cout << "Distance r is: " << r << endl;
    }
};

int main()
{
  point p;
  p.setxandy();
  p.calculateDistance();
  p.display();
}
```

Output

```
Enter x:
4
Enter y:
3
x and y are: 4 and 3
Distance r is: 5
```

College Bus Details List

College has 3 buses. Create an array of objects of class Bus. Class Bus has attributes manufacturer(string), yearofmfg(int), mileage(float). All the 3 buses details should be accepted via input stream cin. Then there should be a method display all bus info to display all bus details.

Also write the expected output for your program execution.

Solution to the above mentioned problem

```cpp
#include <iostream>
using namespace std;
class bus
{
  string manufacturer;
  int yearOfManufacturing;
  float mileage;

public:
  void setBusDetails()
  {
    cout << "Enter Manufaturer:" << endl;
    cin >> manufacturer;
    cout << "Enter year of manufacturing: " << endl;
    cin >> yearOfManufacturing;
    cout << "Enter mileage details: " << endl;
    cin >> mileage;
  }
  void displayBusInfo()
  {
    cout << "Manufacturer :" << manufacturer << endl;
    cout << "Year of manufacturing: " << yearOfManufacturing <<
    endl;
    cout << "Mileage is: " << mileage << endl;
  }
};

int main()
{
  bus buses[3];
  int i = 0;
  for (i = 0; i < 3; i++)
  {
    buses[i].setBusDetails();
  }
  cout << "Bus Details is as follows: " << endl;
  for (i = 0; i < 3; i++)
  {
    buses[i].displayBusInfo();
  }
```

}

Output

```
Enter Manufaturer:
TATA
Enter year of manufacturing:
1999
Enter mileage details:
8
Enter Manufaturer:
Leyland
Enter year of manufacturing:
2000
Enter mileage details:
10
Enter Manufaturer:
Eicher
Enter year of manufacturing:
2001
Enter mileage details:
11
Bus Details is as follows:
Manufacturer :TATA
Year of manufacturing: 1999
Mileage is: 8
Manufacturer :Leyland
Year of manufacturing: 2000
Mileage is: 10
Manufacturer :Eicher
Year of manufacturing: 2001
Mileage is: 11
```

College Department List

Given College has 3 departments. Create an array of objects of class Department. Class Department has attributes specialization(string), yearofinception (int), student count (int). All the department details should be accepted via input stream cin. Then there should be a method display to display all department details.

Also write the expected output for your program execution.

Solution to the above mentioned problem

```cpp
#include <iostream>
using namespace std;
class department
{
    string specialization;
    int yearOfInception;
    int studentCount;

public:
    void setDepartmentDetails()
    {
        cout << "Enter Specialization:" << endl;
        cin >> specialization;
        cout << "Enter year of inception: " << endl;
        cin >> yearOfInception;
        cout << "Enter student count: " << endl;
        cin >> studentCount;
    }
    void displayDepartmentInfo()
    {
        cout << "Specialization :" << specialization << endl;
        cout << "Year of inception: " << yearOfInception << endl;
        cout << "Student count is: " << studentCount << endl;
    }
};

int main()
{
    department departments[3];
    int i = 0;
    for (i = 0; i < 3; i++)
    {
        departments[i].setDepartmentDetails();
```

```cpp
    }
    cout << "Department Details is as follows: " << endl;
    for (i = 0; i < 3; i++)
    {
      departments[i].displayDepartmentInfo();
    }
}
```

Output:

```
Enter Specialization:
CSE
Enter year of inception:
1999
Enter student count:
100
Enter Specialization:
AIML
Enter year of inception:
2006
Enter student count:
200
Enter Specialization:
DataScience
Enter year of inception:
2012
Enter student count:
300
Department Details is as follows:
Specialization :CSE
Year of inception: 1999
Student count is: 100
Specialization :AIML
Year of inception: 2006
Student count is: 200
Specialization :DataScience
Year of inception: 2012
Student count is: 300
```

Chapter 5: Some Moderate Problems Solved

You are hired as a geolocation scientist trainee for a project. The chief researcher assigns you a job of finding shortest distance between any two given points. Each point is characterized by {x,y} cartesian co-ordinates with hypothetical point as a origin. The shortest distance between any two points is given by the following formula:

Shortest distance = $\sqrt{(x2 - x1)^2 + (y2 - y1)^2}$ where (x1,y1) is first point and (x2,y2) is second point.

You must create class Point with x and y as data members. You must respect data encapsulation and data privacy while solving this problem as a seasoned C++ programmer.

Geolocation Problem

Solution to the above problem

```
// Demonstrates
// Functions
// Control structures
// Expressions
// Pointers
```

```cpp
// Classes and Objects
// Blooms Taxonomy Application


#include<iostream>
#include<cmath>
using namespace std;
class Point
{
  private:
  int x,y;
  public:
  Point()
  {
    x=0;
    y=0;
  }
  Point(int x,int y)
  {
    x=x;
    y=y;
  }
  void getxy(int *a, int *b)
  {
    *a = x;
    *b = y;
  }
  void setxy()
  {
    cout<<"Enter cartesian co-ordinates separated by space ";
    cin>>x>>y;
  }
};

int main()
{
  Point p1,p2;
  float shortestDistance=0;
  int x1,y1,x2,y2;
  p1.setxy();
```

CHAPTER 5: SOME MODERATE PROBLEMS SOLVED

```
    p2.setxy();
    p1.getxy(&x1,&y1);
    p2.getxy(&x2,&y2);
    shortestDistance=sqrt((x2-x1)*(x2-x1)+(y2-y1)*(y2-y1));
    cout<<"Shortest distance between Point("<<x1<<","<<y1<<")";
    cout<<"and";
    cout<<"Shortest distance between Point("<<x2<<","<<y2<<")";
    cout<<shortestDistance;
}
```

Output

```
Enter cartesian co-ordinates separated by space 5 2
Enter cartesian co-ordinates separated by space 2 6
Shortest distance between Point(5,2)andPoint(2,6) 5
```

You are given the job of trainee statistician for a day. The chief statistician has assigned you a job of finding the mean, variance and standard deviation from first principles. Meaning, you are not allowed to use built in library functions for statistical calculation of mean, variance and standard deviation. You must create a class DataSet and store the individual values in an integer array and whole array happens to be data member of class Dataset. You must respect data encapsulation and data privacy while solving this problem as a seasoned C++ programmer.
Statistics background:

Mean X_{mean} is $\frac{\sum_1^n xi}{N}$ and Variance = $\sum \frac{(xi - x_{mean})^2}{N}$ and SD = $\sqrt{Variance}$

Statistician Problem Definition

Solution to the above problem

```cpp
// Demonstrates
// Functions
// Control structures
// Expressions
// Classes and Objects
// Blooms Taxonomy Application

#include <iostream>
#include <cmath>
using namespace std;
class DataSet
{
  private:
  int dataset[100];
  float mean,variance,sd;
  public:
  void getDataAndCalculateStats()
  {
    int i=0,m=0;
    float totalVariance=0;
    float sum=0;
    cout<<"How many elements in data set?";
    cin>>m;
    cout<<"Enter the elements individually";
    for(i=0;i<m;i++)
    {
      cin>>dataset[i];
      sum = sum + dataset[i];
    }
    cout <<"sum is"<<sum<<"m is"<<m;
    mean = (sum/m);
    for(i=0;i<m;i++)
    {
      totalVariance = (dataset[i]-mean)*(dataset[i]-mean);
    }
    variance = totalVariance/m;
    sd = sqrt(variance);
  }
```

CHAPTER 5: SOME MODERATE PROBLEMS SOLVED

```
  void printStats()
  {
    cout<<"Mean is "<<mean;
    cout<<"Variance is"<<variance;
    cout<<"SD is"<<sd;
  }
};
int main()
{
  DataSet dataset;
  dataset.getDataAndCalculateStats();
  dataset.printStats();
}
```

Output

```
How many elements in data set?10
Enter the elements individually12 8 11 9 13 7 16 4 15 5
sum is100 Mean is 10 Variance is2.5 SD is1.58114
```

Create a class Arithmetic Progression which has following data members: First element of an array "a", constant difference between successive elements of progression "d" and number of elements in progression "n".

You must have two functions to calculate Sum. One with formula and one without formula.

First function should calculate the sum using following formula $S_n = \frac{n}{2}(2a + (n-1)d)$

Second function should calculate the sum without using the formula by generating the successive terms and adding them using loop.

For given values of a, d and n both functions should generate same Sum. You must respect data encapsulation and data privacy while solving this problem as a seasoned C++ programmer.

Statistician Problem Definition

Solution to the above mentioned problem

```
// Demonstrates
// Functions
// Control structures
// Expressions
// Classes and Objets
// Blooms Taxonomy Application


#include <iostream>
using namespace std;
class ArithmaticProgression
{
  int a,d,n;
  public:
  void setadn()
  {
    cout<<"First term: ";
    cin>>a;
```

```cpp
    cout<<"Constant difference";
    cin>>d;
    cout<<"Number of terms";
    cin>>n;
  }
  int sumUsingFormula()
  {
    int sum =0;
    sum = n/2*(2*a+(n-1)*d);
    cout<<"Sum using formula is "<<sum;
  }
  int sumWithoutFormula()
  {
    int sum = 0;
    int term = a;
    int i=1;
    for(i=1; i<=n;i++)
    {
      sum+=term;
      term = term+d;

    }
    cout<<"Sum without using formula is "<<sum;
  }
};
int main()
{
  ArithmaticProgression ap;
  ap.setadn();
  ap.sumUsingFormula();
  ap.sumWithoutFormula();
}
```

Output:

```
First term: 1
Constant difference2
```

```
Number of terms10
Sum using formula is 100Sum without using formula is 100
```

Chapter 6: Some Pointers Please. Including Copy Constructors

```cpp
#include <iostream>
using namespace std;
int main()
{
  // Declare Data Types
  char a = 'a';
  int b = 10;
  float c = 10.10;
  double d = 14.1234;
  long e = 12345678;

  //Print the initialized values as they are
  cout << "a is " << a << endl;
  cout << "b is " << b << endl;
  cout << "c is " << c << endl;
  cout << "d is " << d << endl;
  cout << "e is " << e << endl;

  // Declare Pointers
  char *pointerToChar;
  int *pointerToInt;
  float *pointerToFloat;
  double *pointerToDouble;
  long *pointerToLong;
```

```cpp
    // Point the Pointers to Respective Data Types
    pointerToChar = &a;
    pointerToInt = &b;
    pointerToFloat = &c;
    pointerToDouble = &d;
    pointerToLong = &e;

    // Print size of data types.
    cout << "size of char is: " << sizeof(char) << endl;
    cout << "size of int is: " << sizeof(int) << endl;
    cout << "size of float is: " << sizeof(float) << endl;
    cout << "size of double is: " << sizeof(double) << endl;
    cout << "size of long is: " << sizeof(long) << endl;

    // Now print size of pointers. The value will be same.
    cout << "size of char pointer is: " << sizeof(pointerToChar) << endl;
    cout << "size of int pointer is: " << sizeof(pointerToInt) << endl;
    cout << "size of float pointer is: " << sizeof(pointerToFloat) << endl;
    cout << "size of int pointer is: " << sizeof(pointerToDouble) << endl;
    cout << "size of float pointer is: " << sizeof(pointerToDouble) << endl;

    // Dereference the pointers and assign different values.
    *pointerToChar = 'b';
    *pointerToInt = 15;
    *pointerToFloat = 15.15;
    *pointerToDouble = 14.87654321;
    *pointerToLong = 87654321;

    // Print the altered values of variables
    cout << "Now a is " << a << endl;
    cout << "Now b is " << b << endl;
    cout << "Now c is " << c << endl;
    cout << "Now d is " << d << endl;
    cout << "Now e is " << e << endl;
}
```

CHAPTER 6: SOME POINTERS PLEASE. INCLUDING COPY CONSTRUCTORS

Above section is introduction to pointers.

Output:

```
a is a
b is 10
c is 10.1
d is 14.1234
e is 12345678
size of char is: 1
size of int is: 4
size of float is: 4
size of double is: 8
size of long is: 4
size of char pointer is: 8
size of int pointer is: 8
size of float pointer is: 8
size of int pointer is: 8
size of float pointer is: 8
Now a is b
Now b is 15
Now c is 15.15
Now d is 14.8765
Now e is 87654321
```

Create a Class person with attributes { name, age, designation and salary}. Create an array of objects of type person. Using pointer of type person iterate through the array once setting the values accepted via input stream and then iterate again displaying the set attributes of the objects. Array size can be assumed as 3.

```
#include <iostream>
using namespace std;
```

```cpp
class Person
{
private:
  std::string name;
  int age;
  std::string designation;
  float salary;

public:

  //set the data using setData
  void setData()
  {
    cout << "Enter the name:" << endl;
    cin >> name;
    cout << "Enter the age:" << endl;
    cin >> age;
    cout << "Enter the designation:" << endl;
    cin >> designation;
    cout << "Enter the salary:" << endl;
    cin >> salary;
  }

  //Display the data using displayDetails
  void displayDetails()
  {
    cout << " Name of the employee is: " << name << endl;
    cout << " Age of the employee is: " << age << endl;
    cout << " Designation of the employee is: " << designation << endl;
    cout << " Salary of the employee is: " << salary << endl;
  }
};
int main()
{
  int i = 0;
  Person listofPersons[3];
  Person *pointerToPerson;
  pointerToPerson = listofPersons;
  //Iterate through the array setting the values
```

CHAPTER 6: SOME POINTERS PLEASE. INCLUDING COPY CONSTRUCTORS

```
    for (i = 0; i < 3; i++)
    {
      pointerToPerson->setData();
      pointerToPerson++;
    }
    // Reinitialize the pointer to start of array again
    // display data of each object of array
    pointerToPerson = listofPersons;
    for (i = 0; i < 3; i++)
    {
      pointerToPerson->displayDetails();
      pointerToPerson++;
    }
}
```

Output:

```
Enter the name:
Abhinandan
Enter the age:
45
Enter the designation:
CTO
Enter the salary:
1000
Enter the name:
Ishan
Enter the age:
16
Enter the designation:
Programmer
Enter the salary:
3000
Enter the name:
Shivansh
Enter the age:
8
```

```
Enter the designation:
Reviewer
Enter the salary:
5000
Name of the employee is: Abhinandan
Age of the employee is: 45
Designation of the employee is: CTO
Salary of the employee is: 1000
Name of the employee is: Ishan
Age of the employee is: 16
Designation of the employee is: Programmer
Salary of the employee is: 3000
Name of the employee is: Shivansh
Age of the employee is: 8
Designation of the employee is: Reviewer
Salary of the employee is: 5000
```

Copy Constructor explained.

CHAPTER 6: SOME POINTERS PLEASE. INCLUDING COPY CONSTRUCTORS

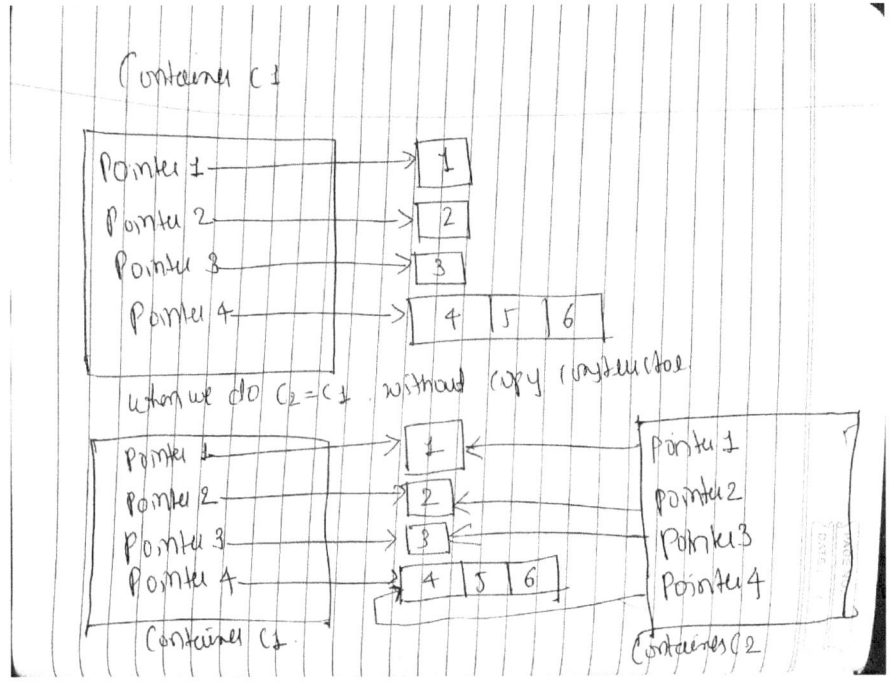

Without Copy Constructor

APPLICATION OF CPLUSPLUS FOR PRACTICAL PROBLEMS

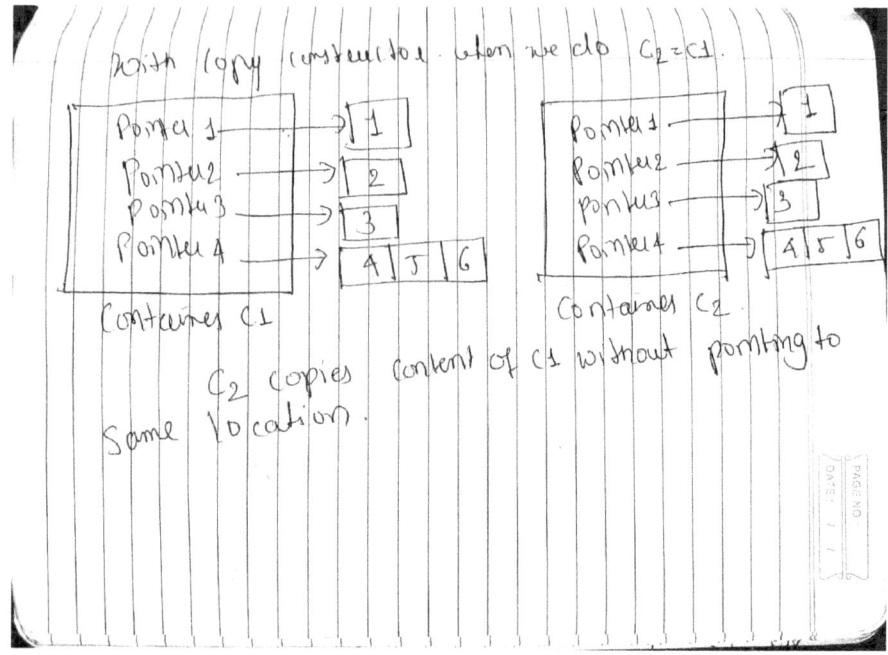

With Proper Copy Constructor

Code below without copy constructor

```
Code below without copy constructor

// Program to demonstrate
// default behaviour of C++ compiler
// where it does bit wise copy when one
// object is assigned to another
// without copy constructor


#include <iostream>
using namespace std;
class container
{
   int arr[3] = {4, 5, 6};
   int *pointer1;
```

CHAPTER 6: SOME POINTERS PLEASE. INCLUDING COPY CONSTRUCTORS

```cpp
    int *pointer2;
    int *pointer3;
    int *pointer4;
public:
    container()
    {
        pointer1 = new int{1};
        pointer2 = new int{2};
        pointer3 = new int{3};
        pointer4 = arr;
    }
    void displayPointerContents()
    {
        cout << "Printing the pointer addresses" << endl;
        int i = 0;
        cout << "Pointer 1 is: " << pointer1 << endl;
        cout << "Pointer 2 is: " << pointer2 << endl;
        cout << "Pointer 3 is: " << pointer3 << endl;
        for (i = 0; i < 3; i++)
        {
            cout << "Pointer4 +" << i << "is: " << pointer4 + i << endl;
        }
    }
    void displayValuePointedByPointers()
    {
        cout << "Printing the values pointed by pointer" << endl;
        int j;
        cout << "pointer1 is pointing to: " << *pointer1 << endl;
        cout << "pointer2 is pointing to: " << *pointer2 << endl;
        cout << "pointer3 is pointing to: " << *pointer3 << endl;
        for (j = 0; j < 3; j++)
        {
            cout<<"pointer4["<<j<<"] is pointing to: ";
            cout << pointer4[j] << endl;
        }
    }
};
int main()
{
```

```
    container c1;
    c1.displayPointerContents();
    c1.displayValuePointedByPointers();
    container c2 = c1;
    c2.displayPointerContents();
    c2.displayValuePointedByPointers();
}
```

Output:

```
Printing the pointer addresses
Pointer 1 is: 0x1db03bcc590
Pointer 2 is: 0x1db03bcc5b0
Pointer 3 is: 0x1db03bc9b70
Pointer4 +0is: 0x531a9ffcc0
Pointer4 +1is: 0x531a9ffcc4
Pointer4 +2is: 0x531a9ffcc8
Printing the values pointed by pointer
pointer1 is pointing to: 1
pointer2 is pointing to: 2
pointer3 is pointing to: 3
pointer4[0] is pointing to: 4
pointer4[1] is pointing to: 5
pointer4[2] is pointing to: 6
Printing the pointer addresses
Pointer 1 is: 0x1db03bcc590
Pointer 2 is: 0x1db03bcc5b0
Pointer 3 is: 0x1db03bc9b70
Pointer4 +0is: 0x531a9ffcc0
Pointer4 +1is: 0x531a9ffcc4
Pointer4 +2is: 0x531a9ffcc8
Printing the values pointed by pointer
pointer1 is pointing to: 1
pointer2 is pointing to: 2
pointer3 is pointing to: 3
pointer4[0] is pointing to: 4
pointer4[1] is pointing to: 5
pointer4[2] is pointing to: 6
```

With Copy Constructor

```cpp
// Program to demonstrate copy constructor
// where default behaviour of C++ compiler
// to do bit wise copy is avoided using
// copy constrcutors.


#include <iostream>
using namespace std;
class container
{
  int arr[3] = {4, 5, 6};
  int *pointer1;
  int *pointer2;
  int *pointer3;
  int *pointer4;

public:
  container()
  {
    pointer1 = new int{1};
    pointer2 = new int{2};
    pointer3 = new int{3};
    pointer4 = arr;
  }
  container(const container &c1)
  {
    int j;
    pointer1 = new int;
    pointer2 = new int;
    pointer3 = new int;
    pointer4 = new int[3];
    *pointer1 = *c1.pointer1;
    *pointer2 = *c1.pointer2;
    *pointer3 = *c1.pointer3;
    for (j = 0; j < 3; j++)
    {
      pointer4[0] = c1.pointer4[0];
```

```cpp
      pointer4[1] = c1.pointer4[1];
      pointer4[2] = c1.pointer4[2];
    }
  }

  void displayPointerContents()
  {
    cout << "Printing the pointer addresses" << endl;
    int i = 0;
    cout << "Pointer 1 is: " << pointer1 << endl;
    cout << "Pointer 2 is: " << pointer2 << endl;
    cout << "Pointer 3 is: " << pointer3 << endl;
    for (i = 0; i < 3; i++)
    {
      cout << "Pointer4 +" << i << "is: " << pointer4 + i << endl;
    }
  }
  void displayValuePointedByPointers()
  {
    cout << "Printing the values pointed by pointer" << endl;
    int j;
    cout << "pointer1 is pointing to: " << *pointer1 << endl;
    cout << "pointer2 is pointing to: " << *pointer2 << endl;
    cout << "pointer3 is pointing to: " << *pointer3 << endl;
    for (j = 0; j < 3; j++)
    {
      cout<<"pointer4["<<j<<"] is pointing to: ";
      cout << pointer4[j] << endl;
    }
  }
};
int main()
{
  container c1;
  c1.displayPointerContents();
  c1.displayValuePointedByPointers();
  container c2 = c1;
  c2.displayPointerContents();
  c2.displayValuePointedByPointers();
}
```

Output:

```
Printing the pointer addresses
Pointer 1 is: 0x15d50cb9bb0
Pointer 2 is: 0x15d50cb9bd0
Pointer 3 is: 0x15d50cb9bf0
Pointer4 +0is: 0x1092bffe50
Pointer4 +1is: 0x1092bffe54
Pointer4 +2is: 0x1092bffe58
Printing the values pointed by pointer
pointer1 is pointing to: 1
pointer2 is pointing to: 2
pointer3 is pointing to: 3
pointer4[0] is pointing to: 4
pointer4[1] is pointing to: 5
pointer4[2] is pointing to: 6
Printing the pointer addresses
Pointer 1 is: 0x15d50cb7af0
Pointer 2 is: 0x15d50cb7b10
Pointer 3 is: 0x15d50cb7b30
Pointer4 +0is: 0x15d50cbf6f0
Pointer4 +1is: 0x15d50cbf6f4
Pointer4 +2is: 0x15d50cbf6f8
Printing the values pointed by pointer
pointer1 is pointing to: 1
pointer2 is pointing to: 2
pointer3 is pointing to: 3
pointer4[0] is pointing to: 4
pointer4[1] is pointing to: 5
pointer4[2] is pointing to: 6
```

Observe the **pointer addresses** in each case.

Chapter 7: Inheritance, Virtual Functions and Run Time Polymorphism

Come up with a program to demonstrate inheritance. In the program Light Motor Vehicle should be inherited from Class Vehicle. Vehicle should have attributes { Make, Year of manufacture, Registration number, Mileage}. The inherited class Light Motor Vehicle should have additional attribute {Infant Passengers Count}. Both base and inherited classes should have constructors to set the values and also they should have setData() functions. There should be displayData() function in base and derived classes to display the attribute values.

Solution:

```
#include <iostream>
using namespace std;
class Vehicle
{
protected:
  std::string make;
  int yearOfManufature;
  std::string registrationNum;
  float mileage;

public:
```

```cpp
  Vehicle(std::string makeVal, int yearOfManufatureVal,
  std::string registrationNumVal, float mileageVal)
    : make{makeVal}, yearOfManufature{yearOfManufatureVal},
      registrationNum{registrationNumVal}, mileage{mileageVal}
  {
  }
  void setData(std::string makeVal, int yesrOfManufatureVal,
  std::string registrationNumVal, float mileageVal)
  {
    make = makeVal;
    yearOfManufature = yesrOfManufatureVal;
    registrationNum = registrationNumVal;
    mileage = mileageVal;
  }
  void displayData()
  {
    cout << "Make of the vehicle is: " << make << endl;
    cout << "Year of manufature is: " << yearOfManufature << endl;
    cout << "Registration number is: " << registrationNum << endl;
    cout << "Mileage is: " << mileage << endl;
  }
};
class LightMotorVehicle : public Vehicle
{
  int infantPassengers;

public:
  LightMotorVehicle(std::string makeVal, int yesrOfManufatureVal,
          std::string registrationNumVal, float mileageVal, int
          infantPassengerVal)
    : Vehicle{makeVal, yearOfManufatureVal, registrationNumVal,
    mileageVal}, infantPassengers{infantPassengerVal}
  {
  }
  void setData(std::string makeVal, int yearOfManufatureVal,
  std::string registrationNumVal, float mileageVal, int
  infantPassengerVal)
  {
    make = makeVal;
    yearOfManufature = yearOfManufatureVal;
```

```cpp
      registrationNum = registrationNumVal;
      mileage = mileageVal;
      infantPassengers = infantPassengerVal;
    }
    void displayData()
    {
      cout << "Make of the vehicle is: " << make << endl;
      cout << "Year of manufacture is: " << yearOfManufature << endl;
      cout << "Registration number is: " << registrationNum << endl;
      cout << "Mileage is: " << mileage << endl;
      cout << "The number of infants allowed: " << infantPassengers
        << endl;
    }
};

int main()
{
  Vehicle v1("TVS", 1999, "KA02C1234", 70.0);
  LightMotorVehicle lmv("TataIndigo", 2013, "KA04C3922", 13.5, 2);
  v1.displayData();
  lmv.displayData();
  v1.setData("Honda", 2003, "KA04C1564", 90);
  lmv.setData("HondaCivic", 2009, "KA05C5678", 23, 2);
  v1.displayData();
  lmv.displayData();
}
```

Output:

```
Make of the vehicle is: TVS
Year of manufature is: 1999
Registration number is: KA02C1234
Mileage is: 70
Make of the vehicle is: TataIndigo
Year of manufacture is: 2013
Registration number is: KA04C3922
Mileage is: 13.5
The number of infants allowed: 2
```

```
Make of the vehicle is: Honda
Year of manufature is: 2003
Registration number is: KA04C1564
Mileage is: 90
Make of the vehicle is: HondaCivic
Year of manufacture is: 2009
Registration number is: KA05C5678
Mileage is: 23
The number of infants allowed: 2
```

Come up with a program to demonstrate Multi Level Inheritance. In the program Light Motor Vehicle should be inherited from Class Vehicle. Super Utility Vehicle should inherit from Light Motor Vehicle. Vehicle should have attributes { Make, Year of manufacture, Registration number, Mileage}. The inherited class Light Motor Vehicle should have additional attribute {Infant Passengers Count}. The Super Utility Vehicle derived from Light Motor Vehicle should have {Infotainment-Manufacturer}. All three classes should have constructors to set the values and also they should have setData() functions. There should be displayData() function in all three classes to display the attribute values.

Solution:

```cpp
#include <iostream>
using namespace std;
class Vehicle
{
protected:
  std::string make;
  int yearOfManufature;
  std::string registrationNum;
  float mileage;
```

```cpp
public:
  Vehicle(std::string makeVal, int yearOfManufatureVal,
  std::string registrationNumVal, float mileageVal)
    : make{makeVal}, yearOfManufature{yearOfManufatureVal},
    registrationNum{registrationNumVal},
     mileage{mileageVal}
  {
  }
  void setData(std::string makeVal, int yesrOfManufatureVal,
  std::string registrationNumVal, float mileageVal)
  {
    make = makeVal;
    yearOfManufature = yesrOfManufatureVal;
    registrationNum = registrationNumVal;
    mileage = mileageVal;
  }
  void displayData()
  {
    cout << "Make of the vehicle is: " << make << endl;
    cout << "Year of manufature is: " << yearOfManufature << endl;
    cout << "Registration number is: " << registrationNum << endl;
    cout << "Mileage is: " << mileage << endl;
  }
};
class LightMotorVehicle : public Vehicle
{
protected:
  int infantPassengers;

public:
  LightMotorVehicle(std::string makeVal, int yesrOfManufatureVal,
          std::string registrationNumVal, float mileageVal, int
          infantPassengerVal)
    : Vehicle{makeVal, yesrOfManufatureVal, registrationNumVal,
    mileageVal},
     infantPassengers{infantPassengerVal}
  {
  }
  void setData(std::string makeVal, int yearOfManufatureVal,
        std::string registrationNumVal, float mileageVal, int
```

```cpp
            infantPassengerVal)
  {
    make = makeVal;
    yearOfManufature = yearOfManufatureVal;
    registrationNum = registrationNumVal;
    mileage = mileageVal;
    infantPassengers = infantPassengerVal;
  }
  void displayData()
  {
    cout << "Make of the vehicle is: " << make << endl;
    cout << "Year of manufacture is: " << yearOfManufature << endl;
    cout << "Registration number is: " << registrationNum << endl;
    cout << "Mileage is: " << mileage << endl;
    cout << "The number of infants allowed: " << infantPassengers
    << endl;
  }
};

class SuperUtilityVehicle : public LightMotorVehicle
{
  std::string infotainmentManufacturer;

public:
  SuperUtilityVehicle(std::string makeVal, int yesrOfManufatureVal,
            std::string registrationNumVal, float mileageVal, int
            infantPassengerVal,
            std::string infotainmentManufacturer)
    : LightMotorVehicle{makeVal, yesrOfManufatureVal,
    registrationNumVal, mileageVal, infantPassengerVal},
      infotainmentManufacturer{infotainmentManufacturer}

  {
  }
  void setData(std::string makeVal, int yearOfManufatureVal,
  std::string registrationNumVal,
          float mileageVal, int infantPassengerVal, std::string
          infotainmentManufacturer)
  {
    make = makeVal;
```

```cpp
    yearOfManufature = yearOfManufatureVal;
    registrationNum = registrationNumVal;
    mileage = mileageVal;
    infantPassengers = infantPassengerVal;
  }
  void displayData()
  {
    cout << "Make of the vehicle is: " << make << endl;
    cout << "Year of manufacture is: " << yearOfManufature << endl;
    cout << "Registration number is: " << registrationNum << endl;
    cout << "Mileage is: " << mileage << endl;
    cout << "The number of infants allowed: " << infantPassengers
      << endl;
    cout << "Infotainment Manufacturer is: " <<
    infotainmentManufacturer << endl;
  }
};

int main()
{
  Vehicle v1("TVS", 1999, "KA02C1234", 70.0);
  LightMotorVehicle lmv("TataIndigo", 2013, "KA04C3922", 13.5, 2);
  SuperUtilityVehicle suv("HondaCRV", 2021, "KA049742", 8.5, 2,
  "Harman");
  v1.displayData();
  lmv.displayData();
  suv.displayData();
  v1.setData("Honda", 2003, "KA04C1564", 90);
  lmv.setData("HondaCivic", 2009, "KA05C5678", 23, 2);
  suv.setData("Mercedez", 2021, "KA041678", 8, 2, "Harman");
  v1.displayData();
  lmv.displayData();
  suv.displayData();
}
```

Output:

CHAPTER 7: INHERITANCE, VIRTUAL FUNCTIONS AND RUN TIME...

```
Make of the vehicle is: TVS
Year of manufature is: 1999
Registration number is: KA02C1234
Mileage is: 70
Make of the vehicle is: TataIndigo
Year of manufacture is: 2013
Registration number is: KA04C3922
Mileage is: 13.5
The number of infants allowed: 2
Make of the vehicle is: HondaCRV
Year of manufacture is: 2021
Registration number is: KA049742
Mileage is: 8.5
The number of infants allowed: 2
Infotainment Manufacturer is: Harman
Make of the vehicle is: Honda
Year of manufature is: 2003
Registration number is: KA04C1564
Mileage is: 90
Make of the vehicle is: HondaCivic
Year of manufacture is: 2009
Registration number is: KA05C5678
Mileage is: 23
The number of infants allowed: 2
Make of the vehicle is: Mercedez
Year of manufacture is: 2021
Registration number is: KA041678
Mileage is: 8
The number of infants allowed: 2
Infotainment Manufacturer is: Harman
```

Come up with a program to demonstrate Multiple Inheritance. In the program Super Utility Vehicle should inherit from Class Vehicle and Infotainment Manufacturer. Vehicle should have attributes {Make, Year of manufacture, Registration number, Mileage}. Infotainment Class should have additional attribute {Infotainment Manufacturer}. Super Utility Vehicle should give the option to set the values either through constructor or through setData(). Super Utility Vehicle Class should have displayData() to display the attributes inherited using multiple inheritance.

Solution:

```cpp
#include <iostream>
using namespace std;
class Vehicle
{
protected:
  std::string make;
  int yearOfManufature;
  std::string registrationNum;
  float mileage;

public:
  Vehicle(std::string makeVal, int yearOfManufatureVal,
  std::string registrationNumVal, float mileageVal)
    : make{makeVal}, yearOfManufature{yearOfManufatureVal},
    registrationNum{registrationNumVal},
     mileage{mileageVal}
  {
  }
  void setData(std::string makeVal, int yesrOfManufatureVal,
  std::string registrationNumVal, float mileageVal)
  {
    make = makeVal;
    yearOfManufature = yesrOfManufatureVal;
    registrationNum = registrationNumVal;
    mileage = mileageVal;
  }
  void displayData()
  {
    cout << "Make of the vehicle is: " << make << endl;
    cout << "Year of manufature is: " << yearOfManufature << endl;
    cout << "Registration number is: " << registrationNum << endl;
    cout << "Mileage is: " << mileage << endl;
  }
};
```

```cpp
class InfotainmentManufacturer
{
protected:
  std::string infotainmentManufacturer;

public:
  InfotainmentManufacturer(std::string infotainmentManufacturerVal)
    : infotainmentManufacturer{infotainmentManufacturerVal}
  {
  }
  void setData(std::string infotainmentManufacturerVal)
  {
    infotainmentManufacturer = infotainmentManufacturerVal;
  }
  void displayData()
  {
    cout << "Infotainment Manufacturer Is: " <<
    infotainmentManufacturer << endl;
  }
};

class SuperUtilityVehicle : public Vehicle,
InfotainmentManufacturer
{
public:
  SuperUtilityVehicle(std::string makeVal, int yesrOfManufatureVal,
           std::string registrationNumVal, float mileageVal,
           std::string infotainmentManufacturer)
    : Vehicle{makeVal, yesrOfManufatureVal, registrationNumVal,
    mileageVal},
      InfotainmentManufacturer{infotainmentManufacturer}

  {
  }
  void setData(std::string makeVal, int yearOfManufatureVal,
  std::string registrationNumVal,
         float mileageVal, std::string infotainmentManufacturerVal)
  {
    make = makeVal;
    yearOfManufature = yearOfManufatureVal;
```

```cpp
    registrationNum = registrationNumVal;
    mileage = mileageVal;
    infotainmentManufacturer = infotainmentManufacturerVal;
  }
  void displayData()
  {
    cout << "Make of the vehicle is: " << make << endl;
    cout << "Year of manufacture is: " << yearOfManufature << endl;
    cout << "Registration number is: " << registrationNum << endl;
    cout << "Mileage is: " << mileage << endl;
    cout << "Infotainment Manufacturer is: " <<
    infotainmentManufacturer << endl;
  }
};

int main()
{
  SuperUtilityVehicle suv("HondaCRV", 2021, "KA049742", 8.5,
  "Harman");
  suv.displayData();
  suv.setData("Mercedez", 2021, "KA041678", 8, "Harman");
  suv.displayData();
}
```

Output:

```
Make of the vehicle is: HondaCRV
Year of manufacture is: 2021
Registration number is: KA049742
Mileage is: 8.5
Infotainment Manufacturer is: Harman
Make of the vehicle is: Mercedez
Year of manufacture is: 2021
Registration number is: KA041678
Mileage is: 8
Infotainment Manufacturer is: Harman
```

Come up with a program to demonstrate to demonstrate Pointers to objects and Derived Classes. In the program Light Motor Vehicle should be inherited from Class Vehicle. Super Utility Vehicle should inherit from Light Motor Vehicle. Vehicle should have attributes { Make, Year of manufacture, Registration number, Mileage}. The inherited class Light Motor Vehicle should have additional attribute {Infant Passengers Count}. The Super Utility Vehicle derived from Light Motor Vehicle should have {Infotainment-Manufacturer}. All three classes should have constructors to set the values and also they should have setData() functions. There should be displayData() function in all three classes to display the attribute values. Create pointers to level 0 class, level 1 and level 2 class. Using Pointers alter the contents and then print the altered values of objects.

```
#include <iostream>
using namespace std;
class Vehicle
{
protected:
  std::string make;
  int yearOfManufature;
  std::string registrationNum;
  float mileage;

public:
  Vehicle(std::string makeVal, int yearOfManufatureVal,
  std::string registrationNumVal, float mileageVal)
    : make{makeVal}, yearOfManufature{yearOfManufatureVal},
    registrationNum{registrationNumVal},
     milcage{mileageVal}
  {
  }
  void setData(std::string makeVal, int yesrOfManufatureVal,
  std::string registrationNumVal, float mileageVal)
  {
    make = makeVal;
    yearOfManufature = yesrOfManufatureVal;
    registrationNum = registrationNumVal;
```

```cpp
    mileage = mileageVal;
  }
  void displayData()
  {
    cout<<"Inside Vehicle Display Data"<<endl;
    cout << "Make of the vehicle is: " << make << endl;
    cout << "Year of manufature is: " << yearOfManufature << endl;
    cout << "Registration number is: " << registrationNum << endl;
    cout << "Mileage is: " << mileage << endl;
    cout<<endl;
  }
};
class LightMotorVehicle : public Vehicle
{
protected:
  int infantPassengers;

public:
  LightMotorVehicle(std::string makeVal, int yesrOfManufatureVal,
          std::string registrationNumVal, float mileageVal, int
          infantPassengerVal)
    : Vehicle{makeVal, yesrOfManufatureVal, registrationNumVal,
    mileageVal},
      infantPassengers{infantPassengerVal}
  {
  }
  void setData(std::string makeVal, int yearOfManufatureVal,
        std::string registrationNumVal, float mileageVal, int
        infantPassengerVal)
  {
    make = makeVal;
    yearOfManufature = yearOfManufatureVal;
    registrationNum = registrationNumVal;
    mileage = mileageVal;
    infantPassengers = infantPassengerVal;
  }
  void displayData()
  {
    cout << "Inside Light Motor Vehicle Display Data" <<endl;
    cout << "Make of the vehicle is: " << make << endl;
```

```cpp
        cout << "Year of manufacture is: " << yearOfManufature << endl;
        cout << "Registration number is: " << registrationNum << endl;
        cout << "Mileage is: " << mileage << endl;
        cout << "The number of infants allowed: " << infantPassengers
        << endl;
        cout<<endl;
    }
};

class SuperUtilityVehicle : public LightMotorVehicle
{
    std::string infotainmentManufacturer;

public:
    SuperUtilityVehicle(std::string makeVal, int yesrOfManufatureVal,
                std::string registrationNumVal, float mileageVal, int
                infantPassengerVal,
                std::string infotainmentManufacturer)
        : LightMotorVehicle{makeVal, yesrOfManufatureVal,
        registrationNumVal, mileageVal, infantPassengerVal},
         infotainmentManufacturer{infotainmentManufacturer}

    {
    }
    void setData(std::string makeVal, int yearOfManufatureVal,
    std::string registrationNumVal,
            float mileageVal, int infantPassengerVal, std::string
            infotainmentManufacturer)
    {
        make = makeVal;
        yearOfManufature = yearOfManufatureVal;
        registrationNum = registrationNumVal;
        mileage = mileageVal;
        infantPassengers = infantPassengerVal;
    }
    void displayData()
    {
        cout << "Inside Super Utility Vehicle Display Data" <<endl;
        cout << "Make of the vehicle is: " << make << endl;
        cout << "Year of manufacture is: " << yearOfManufature << endl;
```

```cpp
        cout << "Registration number is: " << registrationNum << endl;
        cout << "Mileage is: " << mileage << endl;
        cout << "The number of infants allowed: " << infantPassengers
        << endl;
        cout << "Infotainment Manufacturer is: " <<
        infotainmentManufacturer << endl;
        cout<<endl;
    }
};

int main()
{
    Vehicle *ptrToVehicle;
    LightMotorVehicle *ptrToLightMotorVehicle;
    SuperUtilityVehicle *ptrToSuperUtilityVehicle;

    Vehicle v1("TVS", 1999, "KA02C1234", 70.0);
    LightMotorVehicle lmv("TataIndigo", 2013, "KA04C3922", 13.5, 2);
    SuperUtilityVehicle suv("HondaCRV", 2021, "KA049742", 8.5, 2,
    "Harman");
    v1.displayData();
    lmv.displayData();
    suv.displayData();


    ptrToVehicle = &v1;
    ptrToLightMotorVehicle = &lmv;
    ptrToSuperUtilityVehicle =&suv;


    ptrToVehicle->setData("Honda", 2003, "KA04C1564", 90);
    ptrToLightMotorVehicle->setData("HondaCivic", 2009, "KA05C5678",
    23, 2);
    ptrToSuperUtilityVehicle-> setData("Mercedez", 2021, "KA041678",
    8, 2, "Harman");

    v1.displayData();
    lmv.displayData();
    suv.displayData();
}
```

Output:

```
Inside Vehicle Display Data
Make of the vehicle is: TVS
Year of manufature is: 1999
Registration number is: KA02C1234
Mileage is: 70

Inside Light Motor Vehicle Display Data
Make of the vehicle is: TataIndigo
Year of manufacture is: 2013
Registration number is: KA04C3922
Mileage is: 13.5
The number of infants allowed: 2

Inside Super Utility Vehicle Display Data
Make of the vehicle is: HondaCRV
Year of manufacture is: 2021
Registration number is: KA049742
Mileage is: 8.5
The number of infants allowed: 2
Infotainment Manufacturer is: Harman

Inside Vehicle Display Data
Make of the vehicle is: Honda
Year of manufature is: 2003
Registration number is: KA04C1564
Mileage is: 90

Inside Light Motor Vehicle Display Data
Make of the vehicle is: HondaCivic
Year of manufacture is: 2009
Registration number is: KA05C5678
Mileage is: 23
The number of infants allowed: 2

Inside Super Utility Vehicle Display Data
Make of the vehicle is: Mercedez
Year of manufacture is: 2021
```

```
Registration number is: KA041678
Mileage is: 8
The number of infants allowed: 2
Infotainment Manufacturer is: Harman
```

Create Vehicle Class with attributes { Manufacturer, YearOfManufature} then inherit the Vehicle class to create Light Motor Vehicle and Heavy Motor Vehicle Classes respectively. Light Motor Vehicle should have additional attribute {InfantsAllowed} and Heavy Motor Vehicle should have attribute {CargoCapacity}. WAP using this pointer in this case.

```cpp
#include <iostream>
using namespace std;
class vehicle
{
protected:
  std::string manufacturer;
  int yearOfManufacture;

public:
  virtual void setData(std::string manfacturerVal, int
  yearOfManuctureVal)
  {
    this->manufacturer = manfacturerVal;
    this->yearOfManufacture = yearOfManuctureVal;
  }
  virtual void displayData()
  {
    cout << "Year of Manufacture is: " << this->yearOfManufacture
    << endl;
  }
};
class lightMotorVehicle : public vehicle
{
  int infantsAllowed;
```

```cpp
public:
  void setData(std::string manufacturerVal, int
  yearOfManufactureVal, int infantsAllowedVal)
  {
    this->manufacturer = manufacturerVal;
    this->yearOfManufacture = yearOfManufactureVal;
    this->infantsAllowed = infantsAllowedVal;
  }
  void displayData()
  {
    cout << "Manufacturer is: " << this->manufacturer << endl;
    cout << "Year of Manufacture is: " << this->yearOfManufacture
    << endl;
    cout << "Infants Allowed is: " << this->infantsAllowed << endl;
  }
};
class heavyMotorVehicle : public vehicle
{
  int cargoCapacity;

public:
  void setData(std::string manfaturerVal, int
  yearOfManufactureVal, int cargoCapacityAllowed)
  {
    this->manufacturer = manfaturerVal;
    this->yearOfManufacture = yearOfManufactureVal;
    this->cargoCapacity = cargoCapacityAllowed;
  }
  void displayData()
  {
    cout << "Manufacturer is: " << this->manufacturer << endl;
    cout << "Year of Manufacture is: " << this->yearOfManufacture
    << endl;
    cout << "Cargo Capacity Allowed" << this->cargoCapacity <<
    endl;
  }
};
int main()
{
  lightMotorVehicle lmv;
```

```
  lmv.setData((std::string) "Honda", 1999, 2);
  heavyMotorVehicle hmv;
  hmv.setData((std::string) "TATA", 2023, 10000);

  lmv.displayData();
  hmv.displayData();
}
```

Output:

```
Manufacturer is: Honda
Year of Manufacture is: 1999
Infants Allowed is: 2
Manufacturer is: TATA
Year of Manufacture is: 2023
Cargo Capacity Allowed10000
```

Create Vehicle Class with attributes { Manufacturer, YearOfManufature} then inherit the Vehicle class to create Light Motor Vehicle and Heavy Motor Vehicle Classes respectively. Light Motor Vehicle should have additional attribute {InfantsAllowed} and Heavy Motor Vehicle should have attribute {CargoCapacity}. WAP to demonstrate Run Time Polymorphism using virtual function concepts.

Solution:

```
#include <iostream>
using namespace std;
class vehicle
{
protected:
  std::string manufacturer;
  int yearOfManufacture;
```

```cpp
public:
  virtual void setData(std::string manfacturerVal, int
  yearOfManuctureVal)
  {
    manufacturer = manfacturerVal;
    yearOfManufacture = yearOfManuctureVal;
  }
  virtual void displayData()
  {
    cout << "Year of Manufacture is: " << yearOfManufacture <<
    endl;
  }
};
class lightMotorVehicle : public vehicle
{
  int infantsAllowed;

public:
  void setData(std::string manufacturerVal, int
  yearOfManufactureVal, int infantsAllowedVal)
  {
    manufacturer = manufacturerVal;
    yearOfManufacture = yearOfManufactureVal;
    infantsAllowed = infantsAllowedVal;
  }
  void displayData()
  {
    cout << "Manufacturer is: " << manufacturer << endl;
    cout << "Year of Manufacture is: " << yearOfManufacture <<
    endl;
    cout << "Infants Allowed is: " << infantsAllowed << endl;
  }
};
class heavyMotorVehicle : public vehicle
{
  int cargoCapacity;

public:
  void setData(std::string manfaturerVal, int
```

```cpp
    yearOfManufactureVal, int cargoCapacityAllowed)
    {
      manufacturer = manfaturerVal;
      yearOfManufacture = yearOfManufactureVal;
      cargoCapacity = cargoCapacityAllowed;
    }
    void displayData()
    {
      cout << "Manufacturer is: " << manufacturer << endl;
      cout << "Year of Manufacture is: " << yearOfManufacture << endl;
      cout << "Cargo Capacity Allowed" << cargoCapacity << endl;
    }
};
int main()
{
  vehicle *ptrlmv;
  vehicle *ptrhmv;

  lightMotorVehicle lmv;
  lmv.setData((std::string) "Honda", 1999, 2);
  heavyMotorVehicle hmv;
  hmv.setData((std::string) "TATA", 2023, 10000);

  ptrlmv = &lmv;
  ptrhmv = &hmv;

  ptrlmv->displayData();
  ptrhmv->displayData();
}
```

Output:

```
Manufacturer is: Honda
Year of Manufacture is: 1999
Infants Allowed is: 2
Manufacturer is: TATA
Year of Manufacture is: 2023
Cargo Capacity Allowed10000
```

Create Vehicle Class with attributes { Manufacturer, YearOfManufature} then inherit the Vehicle class to create Light Motor Vehicle and Heavy Motor Vehicle Classes respectively. Light Motor Vehicle should have additional attribute {InfantsAllowed} and Heavy Motor Vehicle should have attribute {CargoCapacity}. Come up with a program to create a pure virtual function maxSpeed() in base class. Also demonstrate that C++ compiler does not allow you to instantiate abstract class containing pure virtual function.

Solution:

```cpp
#include <iostream>
using namespace std;
class vehicle
{
protected:
  std::string manufacturer;
  int yearOfManufacture;

public:
  virtual void maxSpeed() = 0;
  virtual void setData(std::string manfacturerVal, int yearOfManuctureVal)
  {
    manufacturer = manfacturerVal;
    yearOfManufacture = yearOfManuctureVal;
  }
  virtual void displayData()
  {
    cout << "Year of Manufacture is: " << yearOfManufacture << endl;
  }
};
class lightMotorVehicle : public vehicle
{
  int infantsAllowed;

public:
  void maxSpeed()
```

```cpp
    {
      cout << "Max speed is 140 km/hr" << endl;
    }
    void setData(std::string manufacturerVal, int
    yearOfManufactureVal, int infantsAllowedVal)
    {
      manufacturer = manufacturerVal;
      yearOfManufacture = yearOfManufactureVal;
      infantsAllowed = infantsAllowedVal;
    }
    void displayData()
    {
      cout << "Manufacturer is: " << manufacturer << endl;
      cout << "Year of Manufacture is: " << yearOfManufacture <<
      endl;
      cout << "Infants Allowed is: " << infantsAllowed << endl;
    }
};
class heavyMotorVehicle : public vehicle
{
  int cargoCapacity;

public:
    void maxSpeed()
    {
      cout << "Max speed is 70 km/hr" << endl;
    }
    void setData(std::string manfaturerVal, int
    yearOfManufactureVal, int cargoCapacityAllowed)
    {
      manufacturer = manfaturerVal;
      yearOfManufacture = yearOfManufactureVal;
      cargoCapacity = cargoCapacityAllowed;
    }
    void displayData()
    {
      cout << "Manufacturer is: " << manufacturer << endl;
      cout << "Year of Manufacture is: " << yearOfManufacture <<
      endl;
      cout << "Cargo Capacity Allowed" << cargoCapacity << endl;
```

CHAPTER 7: INHERITANCE, VIRTUAL FUNCTIONS AND RUN TIME...

```
  }
};
int main()
{
  vehicle *ptrlmv;
  vehicle *ptrhmv;

  // vehicle vh1; If you uncomment this you should get compilation
  // error as abstract classes cannot be instantiated.

  lightMotorVehicle lmv;
  lmv.setData((std::string) "Honda", 1999, 2);
  heavyMotorVehicle hmv;
  hmv.setData((std::string) "TATA", 2023, 10000);

  ptrlmv = &lmv;
  ptrhmv = &hmv;

  ptrlmv->displayData();
  ptrlmv->maxSpeed();

  ptrhmv->displayData();
  ptrhmv->maxSpeed();
}
```

Output:

```
Manufacturer is: Honda
Year of Manufacture is: 1999
Infants Allowed is: 2
Max speed is 140 km/hr
Manufacturer is: TATA
Year of Manufacture is: 2023
Cargo Capacity Allowed10000
Max speed is 70 km/hr
```

Chapter 8: Where to Go from Here?

Again you can read

1. Modern C++ for Absolute Beginners by Slobodan Dmitrović
2. Clean C++ by Stephan Roth
3. Beginning C++17 or C++20 by Ivor Horton Peter Van Weert
4. Online courses both free(YouTube) and Paid(Such as Udemy)

Design as many problem definitions as you want and solve them.

Ample internet resources are available.

Finally wish you a good luck and happy C++ learning journey.

www.ingramcontent.com/pod-product-compliance
Lightning Source LLC
Chambersburg PA
CBHW070428180526
45158CB00017B/918